Animal Verse

This collection contains poems about all kinds of animals, from the humble pet dogs and cats to lions, camels and coyotes. Not forgetting the birds, reptiles, insects and fish that slither, fly, crawl or swim on this earth. There are poems to make us laugh, poems to give us pleasure, and poems to make us think about the responsibility we have towards the creatures with whom we share this planet.

GW00372783

Animal Verse

Compiled by Raymond Wilson

Illustrated by Tessa Barwick

Beaver Books

A Beaver Book
Published by Arrow Books Limited
62–65 Chandos Place, London WC2N 4NW
An imprint of Century Hutchinson Ltd

London · Melbourne · Sydney · Auckland
Johannesburg and agencies throughout
the world

Beaver edition 1982
Reprinted 1988

Set in Souvenir

Printed and bound in Great Britain by
Cox & Wyman Ltd, Reading

ISBN 0 09 959390 4

Contents

Dem Bones Gona Rise Again!

In come de animals two by two:
Hippopotamus and a kangaroo;
  Dem bones gona rise again!

In come de animals three by three:
Two big cats and a bumble bee;
  Dem bones gona rise again!

In come de animals four by four:
Two through de window, and two through de door;
  Dem bones gona rise again!

In come de animals five by five:
Almost dead and hardly alive;
   Dem bones gona rise again!

In come de animals six by six:
Three wid clubs and three wid sticks;
   Dem bones gona rise again!

In come de animals seven by seven:
Four from hell and de others from heaven;
   Dem bones gona rise again!

In come de animals eight by eight:
Four on time, and de others late;
   Dem bones gona rise again!

In come de animals nine by nine:
Four in front and five behind;
   Dem bones gona rise again!

In come de animals ten by ten:
Five big roosters and five big hens;
   Dem bones gona rise again!

Dem bones gona rise again,
Dem bones gona rise again,
I knows it, Oh! I knows it shuah—
   Dem bones gona rise again!

Unknown

The Mouse in the Wainscot

Hush, Suzanne!
Don't lift your cup.
That breath you heard
Is a mouse getting up.

As the mist that steams
From your milk as you sup,
So soft is the sound
Of a mouse getting up.

There! did you hear
His feet pitter-patter
Lighter than tipping
Of beads on a platter,

And then like a shower
On the window pane
The little feet scampering
Back again?

O falling of feather!
O drift of a leaf!
The mouse in the wainscot
Is dropping asleep.

Ian Serraillier

Anne and the Fieldmouse

We found a mouse in the chalk quarry today
In a circle of stones and empty oil drums
By the fag end of a fire. There had been
A picnic there: he must have been after the crumbs.

Jane saw him first, a flicker of brown fur
In and out of the charred wood and chalk-white.
I saw him last, but not till we'd turned up
Every stone and surprised him into flight,

Though not far — little zigzag spurts from stone
To stone. Once, as he lurked in his hiding-place,
I saw his beady eyes uplifted to mine.
I'd never seen such terror in so small a face.

I watched, amazed and guilty. Beside us suddenly
A heavy pheasant whirred up from the ground,
Scaring us all; and, before we knew it, the mouse
Had broken cover, skimming away without a sound,

Melting into the nettles. We didn't go
Till I'd chalked in capitals on a rusty can:
THERE'S A MOUSE IN THOSE NETTLES. LEAVE
HIM ALONE. NOVEMBER 15th ANNE.

Ian Serraillier

10

The Two Rats

He was a rat, and she was a rat,
  And down in one hole they did dwell,
And both were as black as a witch's cat,
  And they loved one another well.

He had a tail, and she had a tail,
  Both long and curling and fine;
And each said, 'Yours is the finest tail
  In the world excepting mine.'

He smelt the cheese, and she smelt the cheese,
  And they both pronounced it good;
And both remarked it would greatly add
  To the charms of their daily food.

So he ventured out, and she ventured out,
  And I saw them go with pain,
But what befell them I never can tell,
  For they never came back again.

Unknown

The Rat

Strange that you let me come so near
    And send no questing senses out
From eye's dull jelly, shell-pink ear,
    Fierce-whiskered snout.

But clay has hardened in these claws
    And gypsy-like I read too late
In lines scored on your naked paws
    A starry fate.

Even that snake, your tail, hangs dead,
    And as I leave you stiff and still
A death-like quietness has spread
    Across the hill.

Andrew Young

12

Spring

Now the sleeping creatures waken—
 Waken, waken;
Blossoms with soft winds are shaken—
 Shaken, shaken;
Squirrels scamper and the hare
Runs races which the children share
Till their shouting fills the air.

Now the woodland birds are singing—
 Singing, singing;
Over field and orchard winging—
 Winging, winging;
Swift and swallow unaware
Weave such beauty on the air
That the children hush and stare.

Raymond Wilson

To a Squirrel

Come play with me;
Why should you run
Through the shaking tree
As though I'd a gun
To strike you dead?
When all I would do
Is to scratch your head
And let you go.

W. B. Yeats

The Squirrel

Among the fox-red fallen leaves I surprised him.

                          Snap

up the chestnut bole leapt,
the brown leaper, clawing up-swept:
turned on the first bough and scolded me roundly.
That's right, load me with reviling,
spit at me, swear horrible, shame me if you can.
But scared of my smiling
off and up he scurries. Now Jack's up the beanstalk
among the dizzy giants. He skips
along the highest branches, along
tree-fingers slender as string,
fur tail following, to the very tips:
then leaps the aisle—
O fear he fall
a hundred times his little length!
He's over! clings, swings on a spray,
then lightly, the ghost of a mouse, against the sky

                                  traces

for me his runway of rare wonder, races
helter-skelter without pause or break
(I think of the snail — how long would he take?)
on and onward, not done yet—
his errand? some nut-plunder, you bet.
Oh he's gone!
I peer and search and strain for him, but he's gone.
I wait and watch at the giant's feet, among
the fox-red fallen leaves. One drop
of rain lands with a smart tap
on the drum, on parchment leaf. I wait
and wait and shiver and forget. . . .

A fancy: suppose these trees, so ancient, so
venerable, so rock-rooted, suddenly
heaved up their huge elephantine hooves
(O the leaves, how they'd splutter and splash
like a waterfall, a red waterfall) — suppose
they trudged away!
What would the squirrel say?

Ian Serraillier

The Snare

I hear a sudden cry of pain!
There is a rabbit in a snare:
Now I hear that cry again,
But I cannot tell from where.

But I cannot tell from where
He is calling out for aid!
Crying on the frightened air,
Making everything afraid!

Making everything afraid!
Wrinkling up his little face!
As he cries again for aid;
— And I cannot find the place!

And I cannot find the place
Where his paw is in the snare!
Little One! Oh, Little One!
I am searching everywhere!

James Stephens

The Rabbit

(*After Prévert*)

We are going to see the rabbit,
We are going to see the rabbit.
Which rabbit, people say?
Which rabbit, ask the children?
Which rabbit?
The only rabbit,
The only rabbit in England,
Sitting behind a barbed-wire fence
Under the floodlights, neon lights,
Sodium lights,
Nibbling grass
On the only patch of grass
In England, in England
(Except the grass by the hoardings
Which doesn't count.)
We are going to see the rabbit
And we must be there on time.

First we shall go by escalator,
Then we shall go by underground,
And then we shall go by motorway
And then by helicopterway,
And the last ten yards we shall have to go
On foot.

And now we are going
All the way to see the rabbit,
We are nearly there,
We are longing to see it,
And so is the crowd
Which is here in thousands

With mounted policemen
And big loudspeakers
And bands and banners,
And everyone has come a long way.
But soon we shall see it
Sitting and nibbling
The blades of grass
On the only patch of grass
In — but something has gone wrong!
Why is everyone so angry,
Why is everyone jostling
And slanging and complaining?

The rabbit has gone,
Yes, the rabbit has gone.
He has actually burrowed down into the earth
And made himself a warren, under the earth,
Despite all these people.
And what shall we do?
What *can* we do?

It is all a pity, you must be disappointed,
Go home and do something else for today,
Go home again, go home for today.
For you cannot hear the rabbit, under the earth,
Remarking rather sadly to himself, by himself,
As he rests in his warren, under the earth:
'It won't be long, they are bound to come,
They are bound to come and find me, even here.'

Alan Brownjohn

The Rabbit

Not even when the early birds
Danced on my roof with showery feet
Such music as will come from rain—
Not even then could I forget
The rabbit in his hours of pain;
Where, lying in an iron trap,
He cries all through the deafened night—
Until his smiling murderer comes,
To kill him in the morning light.

W. H. Davies

The Bells of Heaven

'Twould ring the bells of Heaven
The wildest peal for years,
If Parson lost his senses
And people came to theirs,
And he and they together
Knelt down with angry prayers
For tamed and shabby tigers,
And dancing dogs and bears,
And wretched, blind pit ponies,
And little hunted hares.

Ralph Hodgson

The Hare

Would rather run up-hill than down-hill;
Would rather look backwards than forwards;
Escapes by going the long way round,
Or by lying still.

Mad? A wild lover,
And a bouncing prize-fighter;
But, a careful mother,
In tussocks of couch-grass
Abandons her leverets.

Wounded, captured, screams
Horribly, like a child;
Is eaten half-putrid, boiled
In its own dark blood;

And is sacred to the Moon,
A type of innocent sacrifice.

John Heath-Stubbs

Interruption to a Journey

The hare we had run over
bounced about the road
on the springing curve
of its spine.

Cornfields breathed in the darkness.
We were going through the darkness and
the breathing cornfields from one
important place to another.

We broke the hare's neck
and made that place, for a moment,
the most important place there was,
where a bowstring was cut
and a bow broken for ever
that had shot itself through so many
darknesses and cornfields.

It was left in that landscape.
It left us in another.

Norman MacCaig

The Encounter

Over the grass a hedgehog came
Questing the air for scents of food
And the cracked twig of danger.
He shuffled near in the gloom. Then stopped.
He was aware of me. I went up,
Bent low to look at him, and saw
His coat of lances pointing to my hand.
What could I do
To show I was no enemy?
I turned him over, inspected his small clenched paws,
His eyes expressionless as glass,
And did not know how I could speak,
By touch or tongue, the language of a friend.

It was a grief to be a friend
Yet to be dumb; to offer peace
And bring the soldiers out. . . .

Clifford Dyment

Hedgehog

Twitching the leaves just where the drainpipe clogs
In ivy leaves and mud, a purposeful
Creature at night about its business. Dogs
Fear his stiff seriousness. He chews away

At beetles, worms, slugs, frogs. Can kill a hen
With one snap of his jaws, can taunt a snake
To death on muscled spines. Old countrymen
Tell tales of hedgehogs sucking a cow dry.

But this one, cramped by houses, fences, walls,
Must have slept here all winter in that heap
Of compost, or have inched by intervals
Through tidy gardens to this ivy bed.

And here, dim-eyed, but ears so sensitive
A voice within the house can make him freeze,
He scuffs the edge of danger; yet can live
Happily in our nights and absences.

A country creature, wary, quiet and shrewd,
He takes the milk we give to him, when we're gone.
At night, our slamming voices must seem crude
To one who sits and waits for silences.

Anthony Thwaite

Take One Home for the Kiddies

On shallow straw, in shadeless glass,
Huddled by empty bowls, they sleep:
No dark, no dam, no earth, no grass—
Mam, get us one of them to keep.

Living toys are something novel,
But it soon wears off somehow.
Fetch the shoebox, fetch the shovel—
Mam, we're playing funerals now.

Philip Larkin

A Cat

She had a name among the children;
But no one loved though someone owned
Her, locked her out of doors at bedtime
And had her kittens duly drowned.

In Spring, nevertheless, this cat
Ate blackbirds, thrushes, nightingales,
And birds of bright voice and plume and flight,
As well as scraps from neighbours' pails.

I loathed and hated her for this;
One speckle on a thrush's breast
Was worth a million such; and yet
She lived long, till God gave her rest.

Edward Thomas

The Lost Cat

She took a last and simple meal when there were
                none to see her steal—
  A jug of cream upon the shelf, a fish prepared for
                dinner;
And now she walks a distant street with delicately
                sandalled feet,
  And no one gives her much to eat or weeps to see
                her thinner.

O my belovèd come again, come back in joy, come
                back in pain,
  To end our searching with a mew, or with a purr
                our grieving;
And you shall have for lunch or tea whatever fish
                swim in the sea
  And all the cream that's meant for me — and not a
                word of thieving!

E. V. Rieu

Kilkenny Cats

There once were two cats of Kilkenny
Each thought there was one cat too many;
So they fought and they fit,
And they scratched and they bit,
Till, excepting their nails
And the tips of their tails,
Instead of two cats there weren't any.

Unknown

Cats

Cats sleep
Anywhere,
Any table,
Any chair,
Top of piano,
Window-ledge,
In the middle,
On the edge,
Open drawer,
Empty shoe,
Anybody's
Lap will do,
Fitted in a
Cardboard box,
In the cupboard
With your frocks—
Anywhere!
They don't care!
Cats sleep
Anywhere.

Eleanor Farjeon

Catalogue

Cats sleep fat and walk thin.
Cats, when they sleep, slump;
When they wake, pull in—
And where the plump's been
There's skin.
Cats walk thin.

Cats wait in a lump,
Jump in a streak.
Cats, when they jump, are sleek
As a grape slipping its skin—
They have technique.
Oh, cats don't creak.
They sneak.

Cats sleep fat.
They spread comfort beneath them
Like a good mat,
As if they picked the place
And then sat.
You walk around one
As if he were the City Hall
After that.

Rosalie Moore

The Singing Cat

It was a little captive cat
    Upon a crowded train
His mistress takes him from his box
    To ease his fretful pain.

She holds him tight upon her knee
    The graceful animal
And all the people look at him
    He is so beautiful.

But oh he pricks and oh he prods
    And turns upon her knee
Then lifteth up his innocent voice
    In plaintive melody.

He lifteth up his innocent voice
    He lifteth up, he singeth
And to each human countenance
    A smile of grace he bringeth.

He lifteth up his innocent paw
    Upon her breast he clingeth
And everybody cries, Behold
    The cat, the cat that singeth.

His lifteth up his innocent voice
    He lifteth up, he singeth
And all the people warm themselves
    In the love his beauty bringeth.

Stevie Smith

The Song of the Jellicles

Jellicle Cats come out tonight,
Jellicle Cats come one come all:
The Jellicle Moon is shining bright—
Jellicles come to the Jellicle Ball.

Jellicle Cats are black and white,
Jellicle Cats are rather small;
Jellicle Cats are merry and bright,
And pleasant to hear when they caterwaul.
Jellicle Cats have cheerful faces,
Jellicle Cats have bright black eyes;
They like to practise their airs and graces
And wait for the Jellicle Moon to rise.

Jellicle Cats develop slowly,
Jellicle Cats are not too big;
Jellicle Cats are roly-poly,
They know how to dance a gavotte and a jig.
Until the Jellicle Moon appears
They make their toilette and take their repose:
Jellicles wash behind their ears,
Jellicles dry between their toes.

Jellicle Cats are white and black,
Jellicle Cats are of moderate size;
Jellicles jump like a jumping-jack,
Jellicle Cats have moonlit eyes.
They're quiet enough in the morning hours,
They're quiet enough in the afternoon,
Reserving their terpsichorean powers
To dance by the light of the Jellicle Moon.

Jellicle Cats are black and white,
Jellicle Cats (as I said) are small;
If it happens to be a stormy night
They will practise a caper or two in the hall.
If it happens the sun is shining bright
You would say they had nothing to do at all;
They are resting and saving themselves to be right
For the Jellicle Moon and the Jellicle Ball.

T. S. Eliot

The Tom-cat

At midnight in the alley
   A Tom-cat comes to wail,
And he chants the hate of a million years
   As he swings his snaky tail.

Malevolent, bony, brindled,
   Tiger and devil and bard,
His eyes are coals from the middle of Hell
   And his heart is black and hard.

He twists and crouches and capers
   And bares his curved sharp claws,
And he sings to the stars of the jungle nights,
   Ere cities were, or laws.

Beast from a world primeval,
   He and his leaping clan,
When the blotched red moon leers over the roofs
   Give voice to their scorn of man.

He will lie on a rug tomorrow
   And lick his silky fur,
And veil the brute in his yellow eyes
   And play he's tame, and purr.

But at midnight in the alley
   He will crouch again and wail,
And beat the time for his demon's song
   With a swing of his demon's tail.

Don Marquis

On a Cat, Ageing

He blinks upon the hearth-rug,
   And yawns in deep content,
Accepting all the comforts
   That Providence has sent.

Louder he purrs and louder,
   In one glad hymn of praise
For all the night's adventures,
   For quiet restful days.

Life will go on for ever,
   With all that cat can wish;
Warmth and the glad procession
   Of fish and milk and fish.

Only – the thought disturbs him –
   He's noticed once or twice,
The times are somehow breeding
   A nimbler race of mice.

Alexander Gray

Five Eyes

In Hans' old Mill his three black cats
Watch his bins for the thieving rats.
Whisker and claw, they crouch in the night,
Their five eyes smouldering green and bright:
Squeaks from the flour sacks, squeaks from where
The cold wind stirs on the empty stair,
Squeaking and scampering, everywhere.
Then down they pounce, now in, now out,
At whisking tail, and sniffing snout;
While lean old Hans he snores away
Till peep of light at break of day;
Then up he climbs to his creaking mill,
Out come his cats all grey with meal—
Jekkel, and Jessup, and one-eyed Jill.

Walter de la Mare

The Bloodhound

I am the dog world's best detective.
My sleuthing nose is so effective
I sniff the guilty at a distance
And then they lead a doomed existence.
My well-known record for convictions
Has earned me lots of maledictions
From those whose trail of crime I scented
And sent to prison, unlamented.
Folks either must avoid temptation
Or face my nasal accusation.

Edward Anthony

Mick

Mick my mongrel-O
Lives in a bungalow,
Painted green with a round doorway.
With an eye for cats
And a nose for rats
He lies on his threshold half the day.
He buries his bones
By the rockery stones,
And never, oh never, forgets the place.
Ragged and thin
From his tail to his chin,
He looks at you with a sideways face.
Dusty and brownish,
Wicked and clownish,
He'll win no prize at the County Show.
But throw him a stick,
And up jumps Mick,
And right through the flower-beds see him go!

James Reeves

Family Holiday

Eight months ago, on Christmas Day,
he was a present for the twins,
a toy to join in all their play.

They left by car, but how long since
he cannot tell, nor when they'll come
(if ever) back, to make amends.

The house is blind and deaf and dumb,
the curtains drawn, the windows shut,
the doors sealed tighter than a tomb.

Even the little garden hut
is padlocked. He barks feebly at
each slowing car or passing foot.

Stretched on the WELCOME on the mat
in the front porch, he feels the hunger
gnawing inside him like a rat.

Suffers, endures, but knows no anger.

Raymond Wilson

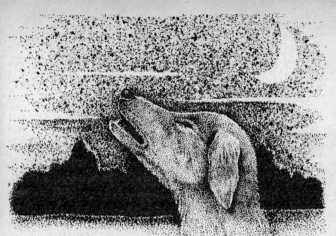

Night Song

On moony nights the dogs bark shrill
Down the valley and up the hill.

There's one who is angry to behold
The moon so unafraid and cold,
That makes the earth as bright as day,
But yet unhappy, dead, and grey.

Another in his strawy lair,
Says: 'Who's a-howling over there?
By heavens I will stop him soon
From interfering with the moon.'

So back he barks, with throat upthrown;
'You leave our moon, our moon alone.'
And other distant dogs respond
Beyond the fields, beyond, beyond.

Frances Cornford

Coyote

Blown out of the prairie in twilight and dew,
Half bold and half timid, yet lazy all through;
Loth ever to leave, and yet fearful to stay,
He limps in the clearing, — an outcast in grey.

A shade on the stubble, a ghost by the wall,
Now leaping, now limping, now risking a fall,
Lop-eared and large-jointed, but ever alway
A thoroughly vagabond outcast in grey.

Here, Carlo, old fellow, he's one of your kind,—
Go seek him, and bring him in out of the wind.
What! snarling, my Carlo! So — even dogs may
Deny their own kin in the outcast in grey.

Well, take what you will, — though it be on the sly,
Marauding or begging, — I shall not ask why;
But will call it a dole, just to help on his way
A four-footed friar in orders of grey!

Bret Harte

Fox

Exploiter of the shadows
He moved among the fences,
A strip of action coiling
Around his farmyard fancies.

With shouting, fields are shaken;
The spinneys give no shelter:
There is delight for riders,
For hounds a tooth in shoulder.

The creature tense with wildness
Knows death is sudden falling
From fury into weary
Surrendering of feeling.

Clifford Dyment

Old Wolf

Lopes on purpose, paddling the snow
Of the soft-blown winterlocked landscape,
Under the loaded branches in the hush of forests.
Stops for its own reasons, shapeless
In the white shadows that have
Stopped breathing.
The prints run into the dark and
The stars wheel, circling the silence.

James Taylor

A Fox Jumped Up

A fox jumped up on a moonlight night,
The stars were shining and all things bright:
'Oh, oh!' said the fox, 'it's a very fine night
For me to go through the town, heigho!'

The fox when he came to yonder stile,
He lifted his ears, and he listened awhile;
'Oh, oh!' said the fox, ''tis but a short mile
From this to yonder town, heigho!'

The fox, when he came to the farmer's gate,
Whom should he see but the farmer's drake?
'I love you too well for your master's sake,
And I long to be picking your bones, heigho!'

The grey goose she ran around the haystack,
'Oh, oh!' said the fox, 'you are very fat,
And you'll do very well to ride on my back
From this to yonder town, heigho!'

The farmer's wife she jumped out of bed,
And out of the window she popped her head,
And she cried 'Oh, husband! the geese are all dead,
For the fox has been through the town, heigho!'

The farmer loaded his pistol with lead,
And shot the old rogue of a fox through the head.
'Ah, ah!' said the farmer, 'I think you are dead,
And no more will you trouble the town, heigho!'

Unknown

The Badgers

Brocks snuffle from their holt within
A writhen root of black-thorn old,
And moonlight streaks the gashes bold
Of lemon fur from ear to chin,
They stretch and snort and snuff the air,
Then sit, to plan the night's affair.

The neighbours, fox and owl, they heed,
And many whispering scents and sounds
Familiar on their secret rounds,
Then silently make sudden speed,
Paddling away in single file
Adown the eagle fern's dim aisle.

Eden Phillpotts

The Sloth

In moving-slow he has no Peer.
You ask him something in his ear,
He thinks about it for a Year;

And, then, before he says a Word
There, upside down (unlike a Bird),
He will assume that you have Heard—

A most Ex-as-per-at-ing Lug.
But should you call his manner Smug,
He'll sigh and give his Branch a Hug;

Then off again to Sleep he goes,
Still swaying gently by his Toes,
And you just *know* he knows he knows.

Theodore Roethke

The Kangaroo

Old Jumpety-Bumpety-Hop-and-Go-One
Was lying asleep on his side in the sun.
This old kangaroo, he was whisking the flies
(With his long glossy tail) from his ears and his eyes.
Jumpety-Bumpety-Hop-and-Go-One
Was lying asleep on his side in the sun,
Jumpety-Bumpety-Hop!

Unknown

My Mother Saw a Dancing Bear

My mother saw a dancing bear
By the schoolyard, a day in June.
The keeper stood with chain and bar
And whistle-pipe, and played a tune.

And Bruin lifted up its head
And lifted up its dusty feet,
And all the children laughed to see
It caper in the summer heat.

They watched as for the Queen it died.
They watched it march. They watched it halt.
They heard the keeper as he cried,
'Now, roly-poly!' 'Somersault!'

And then, my mother said, there came
The keeper with a begging-cup,
The bear with burning coat of fur,
Shaming the laughter to a stop.

They paid a penny for the dance,
But what they saw was not the show;
Only, in Bruin's aching eyes,
Far-distant forests, and the snow.

Charles Causley

The Lamb

  Little Lamb, who made thee?
  Dost thou know who made thee?
Gave thee life and bid thee feed
By the stream and o'er the mead;
Gave thee clothing of delight,
Softest clothing, woolly, bright;
Gave thee such a tender voice
Making all the vales rejoice?
  Little Lamb, who made thee?
  Dost thou know who made thee?

  Little Lamb, I'll tell thee,
  Little Lamb, I'll tell thee:
He is callèd by thy name,
For he calls himself a Lamb.
He is meek, and he is mild;
He became a little Child:
I a child and thou a lamb,
We are callèd by his name.
  Little Lamb, God bless thee.
  Little Lamb, God bless thee.

William Blake

Sheep

When I was once in Baltimore,
   A man came up to me and cried,
'Come, I have eighteen hundred sheep
   And we sail on Tuesday's tide.'

'If you will sail with me, young man,
   I'll pay you fifty shillings down;
These eighteen hundred sheep I take
   From Baltimore to Glasgow town.'

He paid me fifty shillings down,
   I sailed with eighteen hundred sheep;
We soon had cleared the harbour's mouth,
   We soon were in the salt sea deep.

The first night we were out at sea
   Those sheep were quiet in their mind;
The second night they cried with fear—
   They smelt no pastures in the wind.

They sniffed, poor things, for their green fields,
   They cried so loud I could not sleep:
For fifty thousand shillings down
   I would not sail again with sheep.

W. H. Davies

Sheep in Winter

The sheep get up and make their many tracks
And bear a load of snow upon their backs,
And gnaw the frozen turnip to the ground
With sharp quick bite, and then go noising round
The boy that pecks the turnips all the day
And knocks his hands to keep the cold away
And laps his legs in straw to keep them warm
And hides behind the hedges from the storm.
The sheep, as tame as dogs, go where he goes
And try to shake their fleeces from the snows,
Then leave their frozen meal and wander round
The stubble stack that stands beside the ground,
And lie all night and face the drizzling storm
And shun the hovel where they might be warm.

John Clare

Meeting

As I went home on the old wood road,
    With my basket and lesson book,
A deer came out of the tall trees
    And down to drink at the brook.

Twilight was all about us,
    Twilight and tree on tree;
I looked straight into its great, strange eyes,
    And the deer looked back at me.

Beautiful, brown, and unafraid,
    Those eyes returned my stare;
And something with neither sound nor name
    Passed between us there.

Something I shall not forget—
    Something still, and shy, and wise—
In the dimness of the woods
    From a pair of gold-flecked eyes.

Rachel Field

Out in the Dark

Out in the dark over the snow
The fallow fawns invisible go
With the fallow doe;
And the winds blow
Fast as the stars are slow.

Stealthily the dark haunts round
And, when the lamp goes, without sound
At a swifter bound
Than the swiftest hound,
Arrives, and all else is drowned;

And I and star and wind and deer,
Are in the dark together, — near,
Yet far, — and fear
Drums on my ear
In that sage company drear.

How weak and little is the light,
All the universe of sight,
Love and delight,
Before the might,
If you love it not, of night.

Edward Thomas

The Fallow Deer at the Lonely House

One without looks in tonight
   Through the curtain-chink
From the sheet of glistening white;
One without looks in tonight
   As we sit and think
   By the fender-brink.

We do not discern those eyes
   Watching in the snow;
Lit by lamps of rosy dyes
We do not discern those eyes
   Wondering, aglow,
   Fourfooted, tiptoe.

Thomas Hardy

from Horses

The waggons creak and judder down the driftway
To the fields; the teams have their morning bait
And have been groomed. The brasswork clinks and
gleams
On Boxer, the chestnut, leading horse of all.
He is the youngest of the three, and wears
A white star on his tossing well-set head.
It is not long since he was with the colts,
Racing and biting on the pightle grass,
Or gazing wide-eyed at the passers-by,
Until the time came for him to be shod.
Then he was yoked to plough till bever-time,
And brought back home to rest while others worked,
Until the day when he could stand alone.
At harvest carting-time he has the trick
His mother had of drawing to the thraves,
And eating out the heads of sheaves of corn.

H. H. Abbott

Horses

Horses stand up still on the skyline,
Waiting for something to happen;
Strangely thoughtful with big sad eyes,
Watching the rain fall mistily,
The clouds move, or just the distance
Escaping from them.
Horses gallop sometimes — up hills,
Across fields, thundering wild,
In a mad explosion of power;
Hot, steaming, violently animal,
But specially, individually horse.
They flail the air and the ground,
Hard-stiff on legs bone-right
And solid-hooved of nail and iron.
They fetlock thrash the tufts of grass and hair,
Rioting down bone and sinew,
Hurrying to be there.
Gigantically gentle with children,
They feel friendly to the touch,
And take sugar quietly.
Stallion-proud and still they look back
To their primeval youth.
They have learned to be patient.

Paddy Kinsale

The Horse

Hast thou given the horse strength? hast thou clothed
his neck with thunder?
Canst thou make him afraid as a grasshopper? the
glory of his nostrils is terrible.
He paweth in the valley, and rejoiceth in his strength:
he goeth on to meet the armed men.
He mocketh at fear, and is not affrighted; neither
turneth he back from the sword.
The quiver rattleth against him, the glittering spear
and the shield.
He swalloweth the ground with fierceness and rage;
neither believeth he that it is the sound of the trumpet.
He saith among the trumpets, Ha, Ha; and he
smelleth the battle afar off, the thunder of the
captains, and the shouting.

The Book of Job

The Runaway

Once when the snow of the year was beginning to
                                                    fall,
We stopped by a mountain pasture to say, 'Whose
                                                    colt?'
A little Morgan had one forefoot on the wall,
The other curled at his breast. He dipped his head
And snorted at us. And then he had to bolt.
We heard the miniature thunder where he fled,
And we saw him, or thought we saw him, dim and
                                                    grey,
Like a shadow against the curtain of falling flakes.
'I think the little fellow's afraid of the snow.
He isn't winter-broken. It isn't play
With the little fellow at all. He's running away.
I doubt if even his mother could tell him, "Sakes,
It's only weather." He'd think she didn't know!
Where is his mother? He can't be out alone.'
And now he comes again with clatter of stone,
And mounts the wall again with whited eyes
And all his tail that isn't hair up straight.
He shudders his coat as if to throw off flies.
'Whoever it is that leaves him out so late,
When other creatures have gone to stall and bin,
Ought to be told to come and take him in.'

Robert Frost

The Zebras

From the dark woods that breathe of fallen showers,
Harnessed with level rays in golden reins,
The zebras draw the dawn across the plains
Wading knee-deep among the scarlet flowers.
The sunlight, zithering their flanks with fire,
Flashes between the shadows as they pass
Barred with electric tremors through the grass
Like wind along the gold strings of a lyre.

Into the flushed air snorting rosy plumes
That smoulder round their feet in drifting fumes,
With dove-like voices call the distant fillies,
While round the herds the stallion wheels his flight,
Engine of beauty volted with delight,
To roll his mare among the trampled lilies.

Roy Campbell

A Memory

This I remember,
I saw from a train
A shaggy wild pony
That stood in the rain.

Where I was going,
And where was the train,
I cannot remember,
I cannot explain.

All these years after
It comes back again:
A shaggy wild pony
That stood in the rain.

Douglas Gibson

The Donkey

When fishes flew and forests walked
   And figs grew upon the thorn,
Some moment when the moon was blood
   Then surely I was born;

With monstrous head and sickening cry
   And ears like errant wings,
The devil's walking parody
   On all four-footed things.

The tattered outlaw of the earth,
   Of ancient crooked will;
Starve, scourge, deride me; I am dumb,
   I keep my secret still.

Fools! For I also had my hour;
   One far fierce hour and sweet:
There was a shout about my ears,
   And palms before my feet.

G. K. Chesterton

Cow in Calf

It seems she has swallowed a barrel.
From forelegs to haunches
her belly is slung like a hammock.

Slapping her out of the byre is like slapping
a great bag of seed. My hand
tingled as if strapped, but I had to
hit her again and again and
heard the blows plump like a depth-charge
far in her gut.

The udder grows. Windbags
of bagpipes are crammed there
to drone in her lowing.
Her cud and her milk, her heats and her calves
keep coming and going.

Seamus Heaney

Cows

Half the time they munched the grass, and all the time
they lay
Down in the water-meadows, the lazy month of May,
A-chewing,
A-mooing,
To pass the hours away.

'Nice weather,' said the brown cow.
'Ah,' said the white.
'Grass is very tasty.
'Grass is all right.'

Half the time they munched the grass, and all the time
they lay
Down in the water-meadows, the lazy month of May,
A-chewing,
A-mooing,
To pass the hours away.

'Rain coming,' said the brown cow.
'Ah,' said the white.
'Flies is very tiresome.'
'Flies bite.'

Half the time they munched the grass, and all the time
they lay
Down in the water-meadows, the lazy month of May,
A-chewing,
A-mooing,
To pass the hours away.

'Time to go,' said the brown cow.
   'Ah,' said the white.
'Nice chat.' 'Very pleasant.'
   'Night.' 'Night.'

Half the time they munched the grass, and all the time
                           they lay
Down in the water-meadows, the lazy month of May,
     A-chewing,
     A-mooing,
   To pass the hours away.

James Reeves

The Buffalo

Encased in mud, and breathing valley steam,
And teased all day by clouds of stinging flies,
That smother round his flanks and mouth and eyes,
Provoking rage, till an unlidded gleam
Darts from each eye across the sombre stream,
And his great bulk is shaken, to surprise
And scare away the pestering hosts, that rise
Black in the air about him; parrots scream
Above him in the tangled undergrowth,
And monkeys chatter, and the green snake glides
From branch to branch with supple weaving thews,
But he, though irked by noise and stir, is loth
To leave the wallowing-pool that coats his sides
And back and belly with protective ooze.

Herbert Price

The Tiger

Tiger! Tiger! burning bright
In the forests of the night,
What immortal hand or eye
Could frame thy fearful symmetry?

In what distant deeps or skies
Burnt the fire of thine eyes?
On what wings dare he aspire?
What the hand dare seize the fire?

And what shoulder, and what art,
Could twist the sinews of thy heart?
And when thy heart began to beat,
What dread hand? and what dread feet?

What the hammer? what the chain?
In what furnace was thy brain?
What the anvil? what dread grasp
Dare its deadly terrors clasp?

When the stars threw down their spears,
And watered heaven with their tears,
Did He smile His work to see?
Did He who made the Lamb make thee?

Tiger! Tiger! burning bright
In the forests of the night,
What immortal hand or eye
Dare frame thy fearful symmetry?

William Blake

The Tigress

They trapped her in the Indian hills
And put her in a box; and though so young,
The dockers quailed to hear her voice
As she made war on every bolt and thong.

Now she paces, sleeps on her ledge,
Glares, growls, excretes, gnaws lumps of meat,
Sun and shadow in the iron bars
Dropping about her and a listless mate.

Clifford Dyment

The Leopards

One of them was licking the bars of its circus-cage
then gazing out sleepily round the tall tent splendid
just here and there with scarlet and brass,
till the bang of a whip

Brought the animals lolloping onto their chairs (a tail
hung long and twitching, talking its own thoughts).
Possibly the threat was lies, it was not so much
the persuasion

Of the whip, but instead some gipsy trick of the tents
won over these golden kittens to rise and beg
and flaunt their white, powder-puff bellies
(though at the report

Of a lash that curls too near, out flutters a paw
like a discharge from a fuse).
                              Now they are rolling
and cuddling with the bare-chest tamer;
now cowering at the whip-cut.

With humans one judges better; the tamed, the
                                          untamed.
It is harder with these pretenders — claws in, out,
— finally snaking off low to the ground:
yet there was a likeness, something stayed and
                                          haunted
as they bleared and snarled back over their narrow
                                          shoulders
at that whip banging.

Bernard Spencer

60

Lion

Poor prisoner in a cage,
I understand your rage
And why you loudly roar
Walking that stony floor.

Your forest eyes are sad
As wearily you pad
A few yards up and down,
A king without a crown.

Up and down all day,
A wild beast for display,
Or lying in the heat
With sawdust, smells and meat,

Remembering how you chased
Your jungle prey, and raced,
Leaping upon their backs
Along the grassy tracks.

But you are here instead,
Better, perhaps, be dead
Than locked in this dark den;
Forgive us, lion, then,
Who did not ever choose,
Our circuses and zoos.

Leonard Clark

Riverdale Lion

Bound lion, almost blind from meeting their gaze and
                                                popcorn,
the Saturday kids love you. It is their parents
who would paint your mane with polka-dots to match
                                their California shirts
and would trim your nails for tie-clips.

Your few roars delight them. But they wish you
                                would quicken your pace
and not disappear so often into your artificial cave
for there they think you partake of secret joys and
                                                        race
through the jungle-green lair of memory
under an African sun as gold as your mane.

But you fool them. You merely suffer the heat and
                                        scatter the flies
with your tail. You never saw Africa.
Your sign does not tell them that you were born here,
                                        in captivity,
you are as much a Canadian as they are.

                                        John Robert Colombo

The Dromedary

In dreams I see the Dromedary still,
  As once in a gay park I saw him stand:
  A thousand eyes in vulgar wonder scanned
His humps and hairy neck, and gazed their fill
At his lank shanks and mocked with laughter shrill.
  He never moved: and if his Eastern land
  Flashed on his eye with stretches of hot sand,
It wrung no mute appeal from his proud will.
He blinked upon the rabble lazily;
  And still some trace of majesty forlorn
And a coarse grace remained: his head was high,
  Though his gaunt flanks with a great mange were
                                   worn:
There was not any yearning in his eye,
  But on his lips and nostril infinite scorn.

A. Y. Campbell

The Plaint of the Camel

Canary-birds feed on sugar and seed,
    Parrots have crackers to crunch;
And as for the poodles, they tell me the noodles
    Have chicken and cream for their lunch.
But there's never a question
About MY digestion,
    ANYTHING does for me.

Cats, you're aware, can repose in a chair,
    Chickens can roost upon rails;
Puppies are able to sleep in a stable,
    And oysters can slumber in pails.
But no one supposes
A poor Camel dozes,
    ANY PLACE does for me.

Lambs are enclosed where it's never exposed,
    Coops are constructed for hens;
Kittens are treated to houses well heated
    And pigs are protected by pens.
But a Camel comes handy
Wherever it's sandy,
    ANYWHERE does for me.

People would laugh if you rode a giraffe,
    Or mounted the back of an ox;
It's nobody's habit to ride on a rabbit
    Or try to bestraddle a fox.
But as for a Camel, he's
Ridden by families—
    ANY LOAD does for me.

A snake is as round as a hole in the ground;
    Weasels are wavy and sleek;
And no alligator could ever be straighter
    Than lizards that live in a creek.
But a Camel's all lumpy,
And bumpy, and humpy,
    ANY SHAPE does for me.

Charles Edward Carryl

The Llama

The llama is a charmer.
He'll take you by surprise.
He'll pull the wool
Over anyone's eyes!

John L. Foster

The Giraffe

Hide of a leopard and hide of a deer
And eyes of a baby calf,
Sombre and large and crystal clear,
And a comical back that is almost sheer
Has the absurd giraffe.

A crane all covered with hide and hair
Is the aslant giraffe,
So cleverly mottled with many a square
That even the jungle is unaware
Whether a pair or a herd are there,
Or possibly one giraffe,
Or possibly only half.

If you saw him stoop and straddle and drink
He would certainly make you laugh,
He would certainly make you laugh, I think,
With his head right down on the water's brink,
Would the invert giraffe,
The comical knock-kneed, angular, crock-kneed,
Anyhow-built giraffe.

There's more than a grain of common sense
And a husky lot of chaff
In the many and various arguments
About the first giraffe,
The first and worst giraffe;
Whether he grows a neck because
He yearns for the higher shoots
Out of the reach of all and each
Of the ruminating brutes;
Or whether he got to the shoots because

His neck was long, if long it was,
Is the cause of many disputes
Over the ladder without any rungs,
The stopper-like mouth and the longest of tongues
Of the rum and dumb giraffe,
The how-did-you-come giraffe,
The brown equatorial, semi-arboreal
Head-in-the-air giraffe.

Geoffrey Dearmer

Two Performing Elephants

He stands with his forefeet on the drum
and the other, the old one, the pallid hoary female
must creep her great bulk beneath the bridge of him.

On her knees, in utmost caution
all agog, and curling up her trunk
she edges through without upsetting him.
Triumph! the ancient, pig-tailed monster!

When her trick is to climb over him
with what shadow-like slow carefulness
she skims him, sensitive
as shadows from the ages gone and perished
in touching him, and planting her round feet.

While the wispy, modern children, half-afraid
watch silent. The looming of the hoary, far-gone ages
is too much for them.

D. H. Lawrence

The Elephant

Here comes the elephant
Swaying along
With his cargo of children
All singing a song:
To the tinkle of laughter
He goes on his way,
And his cargo of children
Have crowned him with may.

His legs are in leather
And padded his toes;
He can root up an oak
With a whisk of his nose;
With a wave of his trunk
And a turn of his chin
He can pull down a house,
Or pick up a pin.
Beneath his grey forehead
A little eye peers;
Of what is he thinking
Between those wide ears?
What does he feel?
If he wished to tease,
He could twirl his keeper
Over the trees;
If he were not kind,
He could play cup and ball
With Robert and Helen,
And Uncle Paul;

But that grey forehead,
Those crinkled ears,
Have learned to be kind
In a hundred years:
And so with the children
He goes on his way
To the tinkle of laughter
And crowned with the may.

Herbert Asquith

The Hippopotamus

Behold the hippopotamus!
We laugh at how he looks at us,
And yet in moments dank and grim
I wonder how we look to him.
Peace, peace, thou hippopotamus!
We really look all right to us,
As you no doubt delight the eye
Of other hippopotami.

Ogden Nash

Animals in a Museum

Behind the glistening glass
Lifeless in leaping stance,
Their passionate eyes alight
With death's eternal trance,
Or fixed in a frozen snarl,
Powerless to take revenge,
They curse Time's terrible chance
That brought them this dusty end.

Though their fangs no longer strike
At murderous man, I feel
Their eyes pierce to my heart
And my own blood congeal
With the endless moment of death
And the fear that will never pass:
Hunted and hunter alike
Caught in this tomb of glass.

Douglas Gibson

Leviathan

'Canst thou draw out leviathan with an hook?
Or his tongue with a cord which thou lettest down?
Canst thou put an hook into his nose?
Or bore his jaw through with a thorn? . . .
Who can open the doors of his face?
His teeth are terrible round about.
His scales are his pride,
Shut up together as with a close seal. . . .
Out of his mouth go burning lamps,
And sparks of fire leap out.
Out of his nostrils goeth smoke,
As out of a seething pot or cauldron.
His breath kindleth coals,
And a flame goeth out of his mouth. . . .
He maketh the deep to boil like a pot:
He maketh the sea like a pot of ointment.
He maketh a path to shine after him;
One would think the deep to be hoary.
Upon earth there is not his like,
Who is made without fear.
He beholdeth all high things:
He is a king over all the children of pride.'

The Book of Job

Whale

Wouldn't you like to be a whale
And sail serenely by—
An eighty-foot whale from your tip to your tail
And a tiny, briny eye?
Wouldn't you like to wallow
Where nobody says 'Come out!'?
Wouldn't you *love* to swallow
And blow all the brine about?
Wouldn't you like to be always clean
But never to have to wash, I mean,
And wouldn't you love to spout—
   O yes, just think—
A feather of spray as you sail away,
And rise and sink and rise and sink,
And blow all the brine about?

Geoffrey Dearmer

The Whale

Warm and buoyant in his oily mail
Gambols on seas of ice the unwieldy whale,
Wide waving fins round floating islands urge
His bulk gigantic through the troubled surge.

O'er the white wave he lifts his nostril bare,
And spouts transparent columns into the air;
The silvery arches catch the setting beams,
And transient rainbows tremble o'er the streams.

Erasmus Darwin

The Platypus

My child, the Duck-billed Platypus
A sad example sets for us:
From him we learn how indecision
Of character provokes derision.
This vacillating thing, you see,
Could not decide which he would be,
Fish, Flesh, or Fowl, and chose all three.
The scientists were sorely vexed
To classify him; so perplexed
Their brains, that they, with rage at bay,
Called him a horrid name one day,—
A name that baffles, frights and shocks us,
Ornithorhynchus Paradoxus.

Oliver Herford

Bats

A bat is born
Naked and blind and pale.
His mother makes a pocket of her tail
And catches him. He clings to her long fur
By his thumbs and toes and teeth.
And then the mother dances through the night
Doubling and looping, soaring, somersaulting—
Her baby hangs on underneath.
All night, in happiness, she hunts and flies.
Her high sharp cries
Like shining needlepoints of sound
Go out into the night and, echoing back,
Tell her what they have touched.
She hears how far it is, how big it is,
Which way it's going:
She lives by hearing.
The mother eats the moths and gnats she catches
In full flight; in full flight
The mother drinks the water of the pond
She skims across. Her baby hangs on tight.
Her baby drinks the milk she makes him
In moonlight or starlight, in mid-air.
Their single shadow, printed on the moon
Or fluttering across the stars,
Whirls on all night; at daybreak
The tired mother flaps home to her rafter.
The others all are there.
They hang themselves up by their toes,
They wrap themselves in their brown wings.
Bunched upside-down, they sleep in air.

Their sharp ears, their sharp teeth, their quick sharp
                                                   faces
Are dull and slow and mild.
All the bright day, as the mother sleeps,
She folds her wings about her sleeping child.

Randall Jarrell

The Bat

By day the bat is cousin to the mouse.
He likes the attic of an ageing house.

His fingers make a hat about his head.
His pulse beat is so slow we think him dead.

He loops in crazy figures half the night
Among the trees that face the corner light.

But when he brushes up against a screen,
We are afraid of what our eyes have seen:

For something is amiss or out of place
When mice with wings can wear a human face.

Theodore Roethke

Bird and Beast

Did any bird come flying
After Adam and Eve,
When the door was shut against them,
And they sat down to grieve?

I think not Eve's peacock,
Splendid to see.
And I think not Adam's eagle;
But a dove maybe.

Did any beast come pushing
Through the thorny hedge?
Into the thorny, thistly world,
Out from Eden's edge?

I think not a lion,
Though his strength is such;
But I think an innocent lamb
May have done as much.

Christina Rossetti

Cock-crow

Out of the wood of thoughts that grows by night
To be cut down by the sharp axe of light,—
Out of the night, two cocks together crow,
Cleaving the darkness with a silver blow:

And bright before my eyes twin trumpeters stand,
Heralds of splendour, one at either hand,
Each facing each as in a coat of arms:
The milkers lace their boots up at the farms.

Edward Thomas

The Hen and the Carp

   Once, in a roostery,
there lived a speckled hen, and when-
ever she laid an egg this hen
   ecstatically cried:
'O progeny miraculous, particular spectaculous,
   what a wonderful hen am I!'

   Down in a pond near by
perchance a gross and broody carp
was basking, but her ears were sharp—
   she heard Dame Cackle cry:
'O progeny miraculous, particular spectaculous,
   what a wonderful hen am I!'

   'Ah, Cackle,' bubbled she,
'for your single egg, O silly one,
I lay at least a million:
   suppose for each I cried:
"O progeny miraculous, particular spectaculous!"
   what a hullaballoo there'd be!'

Ian Serraillier

The Robin

When up aloft
I fly and fly,
I see in pools
The shining sky,
And a happy bird
Am I, am I!

When I descend
Towards the brink
I stand, and look,
And stoop, and drink,
And bathe my wings,
And chink, and prink.

When winter frost
Makes earth as steel,
I search and search
But find no meal,
And most unhappy
Then I feel.

But when it lasts
And snows still fall,
I get to feel
No grief at all,
For I turn to a cold, stiff
Feathery ball.

Thomas Hardy

A Warning

The robin and the redbreast,
  The robin and the wren,
If you take them out of their nest,
  Ye'll ne'er thrive again.

The robin and the redbreast,
  The martin and the swallow,
If you touch one of their eggs,
  Ill luck is sure to follow.

Unknown

The Red Robin

Cock Robin, he got a new tippet in spring,
And he sat in a shed, and heard other birds sing.
And he whistled a ballad as loud as he could,
And built him a nest of oak leaves by the wood,
And finished it just as the celandine pressed
Like a bright burning blaze, by the edge of its nest
All glittering with sunshine and beautiful rays,
Like high polished brass, or the fire in a blaze;
Then sung a new song on the edge of the brere;
And so it kept singing the whole of the year.
Till cowslips and wild roses blossomed and died,
The red robin sang by the old spinney side.

John Clare

The Caged Bird in Springtime

What can it be,
This curious anxiety?
It is as if I wanted
To fly away from here.

But how absurd!
I have never flown in my life,
And I do not know
What flying means, though I have heard,
Of course, something about it.

Why do I peck the wires of this little cage?
It is the only nest I have ever known.
But I want to build my own,
High in the secret branches of the air.

I cannot quite remember how
It is done, but I know
That what I want to do
Cannot be done here.

I have all I need—
Seed and water, air and light.
Why, then, do I weep with anguish,
And beat my head and my wings
Against these sharp wires, while the children
Smile at each other, saying: 'Hark how he sings'?

James Kirkup

Parrot

The old sick green parrot
High in a dingy cage
Sick with malevolent rage
Beadily glutted his furious *eye*
On the old dark
Chimneys of Noel Park.

Far from his jungle green
Over the seas he came
To the yellow skies, to the dripping rain
To the night of his despair.
And the pavements of his street
Are shining beneath the lamp
With a beauty that's not for one
Born under a tropic sun.

He has croup. His feathered chest
Knows no minute of rest.
High on his perch he sits
And coughs and spits,
Waiting for death to come.
Pray heaven it won't be long.

Stevie Smith

The Red Cockatoo

Sent as a present from Annam—
A red cockatoo.
Coloured like the peach-tree blossom,
Speaking with the speech of men.
And they did to it what is always done
To the learned and eloquent.
They took a cage with stout bars
And shut it up inside.

Po Chu-I
(Translated by Arthur Waley)

Stupidity Street

I saw with open eyes
Singing birds sweet
Sold in the shops
For the people to eat,
Sold in the shops of
Stupidity Street.

I saw in vision
The worm in the wheat,
And in the shops nothing
For people to eat;
Nothing for sale in
Stupidity Street.

Ralph Hodgson

Little Trotty Wagtail

Little Trotty Wagtail, he went in the rain,
And tittering, tottering sideways, he ne'er got straight
again,
He stooped to get a worm, and looked up to catch a
fly,
And then he flew away ere his feathers they were dry.

Little Trotty Wagtail, he waddled in the mud,
And left his little footmarks, trample where he would.
He waddled in the water-pudge, and waggle went his
tail,
And chirrup up his wings to dry upon the garden rail.

Little Trotty Wagtail, you nimble all about,
And in the dimpling water-pudge, you waddle in and
out;
Your home is nigh at hand, and in the warm pigsty,
So, little Master Wagtail, I'll bid you a good-bye.

John Clare

O What if the Fowler

O what if the fowler my blackbird has taken?
  The roses of dawn blossom over the sea;
Awaken, my blackbird, awaken, awaken,
  And sing to me out of my red fuchsia tree!

O what if the fowler my blackbird has taken?
  The sun lifts his head from the lap of the sea—
Awaken, my blackbird, awaken, awaken,
  And sing to me out of my red fuchsia tree!

O what if the fowler my blackbird has taken?
  The mountain grown white with the birds of the
                              sea;
But down in my garden forsaken, forsaken,
  I'll weep all the day by my red fuchsia tree!

Charles Dalmon

Magpie in the Snow

White land
Black veins of branches
Dead blue eye of the sky
Magpie flicks tail
Dances
Winks a living eye.

East wind
Dry bones of branches
Scoured and aching sky
Magpie cocks head
Listens
Views the world awry.

Hard ground
Thin roof of branches
Far unfriendly sky
Magpie cares naught
Chatters
Flings its wings to fly.

Michael Tanner

A Bird Came Down the Walk

A bird came down the walk.
He did not know I saw.
He bit an angleworm in halves
And ate the fellow raw,

And then he drank a dew
From a convenient grass,
And then hopped sidewise to the wall
To let a beetle pass.

He glanced with rapid eyes
That hurried all around;
They looked like frightened beads, I thought;
He stirred his velvet head

Like one in danger, cautious;
I offered him a crumb,
And he unrolled his feathers
And rode him softer home

Than oars divide the ocean,
Too silver for a seam,
Or butterflies off banks of noon
Leap, plashless as they swim.

Emily Dickinson

Pigeons

They paddle with staccato feet
In powder-pools of sunlight,
Small blue busybodies
Strutting like fat gentlemen
With hands clasped
Under their swallowtail coats;
And, as they stump about,
Their heads like tiny hammers
Tap at imaginary nails
In non-existent walls.
Elusive ghosts of sunshine
Slither down the green gloss
Of their necks an instant, and are gone.

Summer hangs drugged from sky to earth
In limpid fathoms of silence:
Only warm dark dimples of sound
Slide like slow bubbles
From the contented throats.

Raise a casual hand—
With one quick gust
They fountain into air.

Richard Kell

A London Sparrow's If

If you c'n keep alive when li'l bleeders
    Come arter y' wi' catapults an' stones;
If you c'n grow up unpertickler feeders,
    An' live on rubbidge, crumbs, an' 'addock bones;
If you c'n nest up in the bloomin' gutters,
    An' dodge the blinkin' tabby on the tiles;
Nip under wheels an' never get the flutters,
    Wear brahn an' no bright-coloured fevver-styles;
If you ain't blown b' nippers (Cor, I'd skin 'em!);
    Stop in y'r shells nah, warm-like, under me;
Yours is the eggs an' everyfink 'at's in 'em—
    An' when they 'atch, your be cock-sparrers, see?

J. A. Lindon

Thames Gulls

    Beautiful it is to see
On London Bridge the bold-eyed seabirds wheel,
And hear them cry, and all for a light-flung crust
Fling us their wealth, their freedom, speed and gleam.
    And beautiful to see
Them that pass by lured by these birds to stay,
And smile and say 'how tame they are' — how tame!
Friendly as stars to steersmen in mid seas,
And as remote as midnight's darling stars,
Pleasant as voices heard from days long done,
As nigh the hand as windflowers in the woods,
And inaccessible as Dido's phantom.

Edmund Blunden

The Cranes

We thought they were gulls at first, while they were
                                                distant—
The two cranes flying out of a normal morning.
They circled twice about our house and sank,
Their long legs drooping, down over the wood.
We saw their wings flash white, frayed at the black tip,
And heard their harsh cry, like a rusty screw.
Down in the next field, shy and angular,
They darted their long necks in the grass for fish.
They would not have us close, but shambled coyly,
Ridiculous, caught on the ground. Yet our fields
Under their feet became a fen; the sky
That was blue July became watery November,
And echoing with the cries of foreign birds.

Anne Ridler

The Heron

On lonely river-mud a heron alone
Of all things moving – water, reeds and mist –
Maintains his sculptured attitude of stone.
A dead leaf floats on the sliding river, kissed
By its own reflection in a brief farewell.
Movement without sound; the evening drifts
On autumn tides of colour, light, and smell
Of warm decay; and now the heron lifts
Enormous wings in elegy; a grey
Shadow that seems to bear the light away.

Phoebe Hesketh

The Heron

The Heron stands in water where the swamp
Has deepened to the blackness of a pool,
Or balances with one leg on a hump
Of marsh grass heaped above a muskrat hole.

He walks the shallow with an antic grace.
The great feet break the ridges of the sand,
The long eye notes the minnows' hiding place.
His beak is quicker than a human hand.

He jerks a frog across his bony lip.
Then points his heavy bill above the wood.
The wide wings flap but once to lift him up.
A single ripple starts from where he stood.

Theodore Roethke

Mallard

Squawking they rise from reeds into the sun,
climbing like furies, running on blood and bone,
with wings like garden shears clipping the misty air,
four mallard, hard winged, with necks like rods
fly in perfect formation over the marsh.

Keeping their distance, gyring, not letting slip the air,
but leaping into it straight like hounds or divers,
they stretch out into the wind and sound their horns
again.

Suddenly siding to a bank of air unbidden
by hand signal or morse message of command
down sky they plane, sliding like corks on a current,
designed so deftly that all air is advantage,

till, with few flaps, orderly as they left earth,
alighting among curlew they pad on mud.

Rex Warner

Ducks' Ditty

All along the backwater,
Through the rushes tall,
Ducks are a-dabbling,
Up tails all!

Ducks' tails, drakes' tails,
Yellow feet a-quiver,
Yellow bills all out of sight
Busy in the river!

Slushy green undergrowth
Where the roach swim—
Here we keep our larder,
Cool and full and dim!

Every one for what he likes!
We like to be
Heads down, tails up,
Dabbling free!

High in the blue above
Swifts whirl and call—
We are down a-dabbling,
Up tails all!

Kenneth Grahame

The Swans

How lovely are these swans,
That float like high proud galleons
Cool in the summer heat,
And waving leaf-like feet
Divide with narrow breasts of snow
In a smooth surge
This water that is mostly sky;
So lovely that I know
Death cannot kill such birds;
It could but wound them, mortally.

Andrew Young

The Swans

Midstream they met. Challenger and Champion,
They fought a war for honour
Fierce, sharp, but with no honour;
Each had a simple aim and sought it quickly.
The combat over, the victor sailed away,
Broken, but placid as is the gift of swans,
Leaving his rival to his shame alone.

I listened for a song, according to story,
But this swan's death was out of character—
No giving up the grace of life
In a sad lingering music.
I saw the beaten swan rise on the water
As though to outreach pain, its webbed feet
Banging the river helplessly, its wings
Loose in a last hysteria. Then the neck
Was floating like a rope and the swan was dead.
It drifted away and all around it swan's down
Bobbed on the river like children's boats.

Clifford Dyment

The Silver Swan

The silver swan, who living had no note,
When death approached, unlocked her silent throat,
Leaning her breast against the reedy shore,
Thus sung her first and last, and sung no more:
Farewell all joys! O death, come close mine eyes;
More geese than swans now live, more fools than
wise.

Unknown

95

Something Told the Wild Geese

Something told the wild geese
It was time to go,
Though the fields lay golden
Something whispered, 'Snow!'
Leaves were green and stirring,
Berries lustre-glossed,
But beneath warm feathers
Something cautioned, 'Frost!'

All the sagging orchards
Steamed with amber spice,
But each wild beast stiffened
At remembered ice.
Something told the wild geese
It was time to fly—
Summer sun was on their wings,
Winter in their cry.

Rachel Field

The Eagle

He hangs between his wings outspread
Level and still
And bends a narrow golden head,
Scanning the ground to kill,

Though as he sails and smoothly swings
Round the hill-side,
He looks as though from his own wings
He hung down crucified.

Andrew Young

The Eagle

He clasps the crag with crooked hands;
Close to the sun in lonely lands,
Ring'd with the azure world, he stands.

The wrinkled sea beneath him crawls;
He watches from his mountain walls,
And like a thunderbolt he falls.

Alfred, Lord Tennyson

Horrible Song

The Crow is a wicked creature
   Crooked in every feature.
Beware, beware of the Crow!
When the bombs burst, he laughs, he shouts;
When the guns go off, he roundabouts;
When the limbs start to fly and the blood starts to flow
   Ho Ho Ho
   He sings the Song of the Crow.

The Crow is a sudden creature
   Thievish in every feature.
Beware, beware of the Crow!
When the sweating farmers sleep
He levers the jewels from the heads of their sheep.
Die in a ditch, your own will go,
   Ho Ho Ho
   While he sings the Song of the Crow.

The Crow is a subtle creature
   Cunning in every feature.
Beware, beware of the Crow!
When sick folk tremble on their cots
He sucks their souls through the chimney pots,
They're dead and gone before they know,
   Ho Ho Ho
   And he sings the Song of the Crow.

The Crow is a lusty creature
    Gleeful in every feature.
Beware, beware of the Crow!
If he can't get your liver, he'll find an old rat
Or highway hedgehog hammered flat,
Any old rubbish to make him grow,
    Ho Ho Ho
    While he sings the Song of the Crow.

The Crow is a hardy creature
    Fire-proof in every feature.
Beware, beware of the Crow!
When Mankind's blasted to kingdom come
The Crow will dance and hop and drum
And into an old thigh-bone he'll blow
    Ho Ho Ho
    Singing the Song of the Crow.

Ted Hughes

from **Summer Evening**

Crows crowd croaking overhead,
Hastening to the woods to bed.
Cooing sits the lonely dove,
Calling home her absent love.
With 'Kirchup! Kirchup!' 'mong the wheats,
Partridge distant partridge greets. . . .

Bats flit by in hood and cowl;
Through the barn-hole pops the owl;
From the hedge, in drowsy hum,
Heedless buzzing beetles bum,
Haunting every bushy place,
Flopping in the labourer's face. . . .

John Clare

Rookery

Here they come, freckling the sunset,
The slow big sailers bearing down
On the plantation. They have flown
Their sorties and are now well met.

The upper twigs dip and wobble
With each almost two-point landing,
Then ride to rest. There is nothing
Else to do now only settle.

But they keep up a guttural chat
As stragglers knock the roost see-saw.
Something's satisfied in that caw.
Who wouldn't come to rest like that?

Seamus Heaney

The Nightingale

On his little twig of plum,
   His plum-tree twig, the nightingale
Dreamed one night that snow had come,
   On the hill and in the vale,
   In the vale and on the hill,
   Everything white and soft and still,
Only the snowflakes falling, falling,
   Only the snow. . . .

On a night when the snow had come,
   As the snowflakes fell the nightingale
Dreamed of orchards white with plum,
   On the hill and in the vale,
   In the vale and on the hill,
   Everything soft and white and still,
Only the petals falling, falling,
   Only the plum. . . .

Ian Colvin
(from a Japanese Nursery Rhyme)

Sweet Suffolk Owl

Sweet Suffolk owl, so trimly dight*
With feathers like a lady bright,
Thou sing'st alone, sitting by night,
   Tu-whit, tu-whoo!

Thy note, that forth so freely rolls,
With shrill command the mouse controls,
And sings a dirge for dying souls,
   Tu-whit, tu-whoo!

Thomas Vautor

* dressed

The Owl and the Pussy-Cat

The Owl and the Pussy-Cat went to sea
In a beautiful pea-green boat,
They took some honey, and plenty of money,
Wrapped up in a five-pound note.
The Owl looked up to the stars above,
And sang to a small guitar,
'O lovely Pussy! O Pussy, my love,
What a beautiful Pussy you are,
              You are,
              You are!
What a beautiful Pussy you are!'

Pussy said to the Owl, 'You elegant fowl!
How charmingly sweet you sing!
O let us be married! too long we have tarried:
But what shall we do for a ring?
They sailed away for a year and a day,
To the land where the Bong-tree grows,
And there in a wood a Piggy-wig stood,
With a ring at the end of his nose.
              His nose,
              His nose,
With a ring at the end of his nose.

'Dear Pig, are you willing to sell for one shilling
Your ring?' Said the Piggy, 'I will.'
So they took it away, and were married next day
By the Turkey who lives on the hill.
They dined on mince, and slices of quince,
Which they ate with a runcible spoon;
And hand in hand, on the edge of the sand,
They danced in the light of the moon,
    The moon,
    The moon,
They danced by the light of the moon.

Edward Lear

The Owl

When cats run home and light is come,
 And dew is cold upon the ground,
And the far-off stream is dumb,
 And the whirring sail goes round,
 And the whirring sail goes round;
  Alone and warming his five wits,
  The white owl in the belfry sits.

When merry milkmaids click the latch,
 And rarely smells the new-mown hay,
And the cock hath sung beneath the thatch
 Twice or thrice his roundelay,
 Twice or thrice his roundelay;
  Alone and warming his five wits,
  The white owl in the belfry sits.

Alfred, Lord Tennyson

The Cat-eyed Owl

The cat-eyed owl, although so fierce
At night with kittens and with mice

In daylight may be mobbed
By flocks of little birds, and in
The market-place, be robbed

Of all his dignity and wisdom
By children market-women and malingering men

Who hoot at it and mocking its myopic
Eyes, shout: 'Look!
Look at it now, he hangs his head in

Shame.' This never happens to the eagle
Or the nightingale.

Edward Brathwaite

Humming-bird

I can imagine, in some otherworld
Primeval-dumb, far back
In that most awful stillness, that only gasped and
                                              hummed,
Humming-birds raced down the avenues.

Before anything had a soul,
While life was a heave of Matter, half inanimate,
This little bit chipped off in brilliance
And went whizzing through the slow, vast, succulent
                                                stems.

I believe there were no flowers then,
In the world where the humming-bird flashed ahead
                                          of creation.
I believe he pierced the slow vegetable veins with his
                                              long beak.

Probably he was big
As mosses, and little lizards, they say, were once big.
Probably he was a jabbing, terrifying monster.

We look at him through the wrong end of the long
                                    telescope of Time,
Luckily for us.

D. H. Lawrence

The Bird

When I got home
Last night I found
A bird the cat
Had brought into the house
On the kitchen floor.

It wasn't dead.
It looked as if
It was, at first.
There were some feathers lying
Against the wall:

The bird itself
With its wings folded
Lay and stared.
It didn't move.
I picked it up:

Quivering like a clockwork
Toy in my hand
I carried it out
Into the yard
And put it down

In a slice of light
From the door. I lifted
A long broom
By the handle near to
The head and struck

The bird four times.
The fourth time it
Didn't move.
Blood, in a stringy
Trickle, blotched

The white concrete.
I edged the remains
Up with a red
Plastic shovel.
Lifting it through

The house to the cellar
I tipped it out
In the dust-bin along with
Snakes of fluff
And empty soup-tins.

When I emptied the tea-leaves
This morning I saw
The bird I killed
Leaning its head
On a broken egg-shell.

George Macbeth

Tortoise

Lumbering carefully over stone and earth,
    Edging, stumbling, groping blindly,
To the favourite place of Michaelmas daisies.
    His food finished, now the tortoise
Feels his way one foot after another,
    Choosing a path among grass,
Which looks like willows hovering high above his
                        hard shell.
    Afternoon appears, sleep overpowers the beast,
Making heavy footsteps the tortoise finds a sleeping-
                        place,
    One eye closes and the scum of the eyelid passes
                        over both eyes,
The tortoise falls into a shelled sleep.
    Dawn; and he trundles off to find food,
He claws his way over the rockery,
    Which appears to him to be like the Andes,
Passing through glades of raspberries;
    And at last he finds his food,
Lettuce!
    Clumsily he opens his leather-hard jaws,
Draws his fire-red tongue out,
    Then, with a churning of cranking and creaking
                        efforts,
He closes his mouth upon the lettuce;
    Tortoise now returns and digs with great speed,
To hide himself from winter.
    The hole dug, he retreats in his creaking wet-
                        covered shell,
To sleep.

David Speechly

Tony the Turtle

Tony was a Turtle,
  Very much at ease,
Swimming in the sunshine
  Through the summer seas,
And feeding on the fishes
Irrespective of their wishes,
With a 'By your leave' and 'Thank you'
  And a gentlemanly squeeze.

Tony was a Turtle
  Who loved a civil phrase;
Anxious and obliging,
  Sensitive to praise.
And to hint that he was snappy
Made him thoroughly unhappy;
For Tony was a Turtle
  With most engaging ways.

Tony was a Turtle
  Who thought, before he fed,
Of other people's comfort,
  And as he ate them said:
'If I seem a little grumpy,
It is *not* that you are lumpy,'
  For Tony was a Turtle
  Delicately bred.

                    E. V. Rieu

If You Should Meet a Crocodile

If you should meet a crocodile,
 Don't take a stick and poke him;
Ignore the welcome in his smile,
 Be careful not to stroke him.
For as he sleeps upon the Nile,
 He thinner gets and thinner;
And whene'er you meet a crocodile
 He's ready for his dinner.

       Unknown

A Lobster Quadrille

'Will you walk a little faster?' said a whiting to a snail,
'There's a porpoise close behind us, and he's
         treading on my tail.
See how eagerly the lobsters and the turtles all
           advance!
They are waiting on the shingle — will you come and
        join the dance?
Will you, won't you, will you, won't you, will you join
        the dance?
Will you, won't you, will you, won't you, won't you
        join the dance?

'You can really have no notion how delightful it will
                                                    be
When they take us up and throw us, with the
                                    lobsters, out to sea!'
But the snail replied, 'Too far, too far!' and gave a look
                                    askance—
Said he thanked the whiting kindly, but he would not
                                    join the dance.
Would not, could not, would not, could not, would
                                    not join the dance.
Would not, could not, would not, could not, could
                                    not join the dance.

'What matters it how far we go?' his scaly friend
                                    replied,
'There is another shore, you know, upon the other
                                    side.
The further off from England the nearer is to
                                    France—
Then turn not pale, beloved snail, but come and join
                                    the dance.
Will you, won't you, will you, won't you, will you join
                                    the dance?
Will you, won't you, will you, won't you, won't you
                                    join the dance?'

Lewis Carroll

The Dead Crab

A rosy shield upon its back
That not the hardest storm could crack,
From whose sharp edge projected out
Black pin-point eyes staring about;
Beneath, the well-knit cote-armure
That gave to its weak belly power;
The clustered legs with plated joints
That ended in stiletto points;
The claws like mouths it held outside:—
I cannot think this creature died
By storm or fish or sea-fowl harmed
Walking the sea so heavily armed;
Or does it make for death to be
Oneself a living armoury?

Andrew Young

114

Skate

Flitting the sea-bed, wide and flat,
I am a fish to wonder at:

A kind of, sort of, soft thick square,
Like a slow plane in watery air,

With a tough white spine from tail to lips
And straight bones out to my side-wing-tips,

No other interests interest me,
Being this is my whole activity.

Alan Brownjohn

Minnows

Swarms of minnows show their little heads,
Staying their wavy bodies 'gainst the streams,
To taste the luxury of sunny beams
Tempered with coolness. How they ever wrestle
With their own sweet delight, and ever nestle
Their silver bellies on the pebbly sand.
If you but scantily hold out the hand,
That very instant not one will remain;
But turn your eye, and they are there again.

John Keats

Fish

Look at the fish!
Look at the fish!
Look at the fish that is blue and green!
Look at the fish that is tangerine!
Look at the fish that is gold and black
With monocled eye and a big humpback!
Look at the fish with a ring in its nose,
And a mouth he cannot open or close!
Look at the fish with lavender stripes
And long front teeth like organ pipes,
And fins that are finer than Irish lace.
Look at the funny grin on his face,
Look at him swimming all over the place!
Look at the fish!
Look at the fish!
Look at the fish
They're so *beautiful.*

William Jay Smith

Goldfish

One small fish in a
Polythene bag;
Can't swim round, can
Only look sad.
Take a pair of scissors,
Snip a quick hole,
Down flops water
And fish into a bowl!

She waits a little moment,
Flips her tail free,
Then off into circles
As frisk as can be.
Dash-about — splash-about—
Do what you wish:
You're mine, you black-spotted
Cheeky-eyed
Fish!

John Walsh

The Goldfish

Lazily through the clear
Shallow and deep,
He oars his chartless way,
Half-asleep,
The little paradox — so bright — so cold,
Although his flesh seems formed of fire and gold.

High emperor of his dim
Bubble-empearled
Jet-shadowed greenish-shallowed
Water-world—
Like a live torch, a brand of burning gold,
He sets the wave afire and still is cold.

A. A. Brown

At the Aquarium

Serene the silver fishes glide,
Stern-lipped and pale, and wonder-eyed;
As through the agèd deeps of ocean,
They glide with wan and wavy motion.
They have no pathway where they go,
They flow like water to and fro.
They watch with never-winking eyes,
They watch with staring, cold surprise,
The level people in the air,
The people peering, peering there,
Who wander also to and fro,
And know not why or where they go,
Yet have a wonder in their eyes,
Sometimes a pale and cold surprise.

Max Eastman

The Shark

He seemed to know the harbour,
So leisurely he swam;
His fin,
Like a piece of sheet-iron,
Three-cornered,
And with knife-edge,
Stirred not a bubble
As it moved
With its base-line on the water.

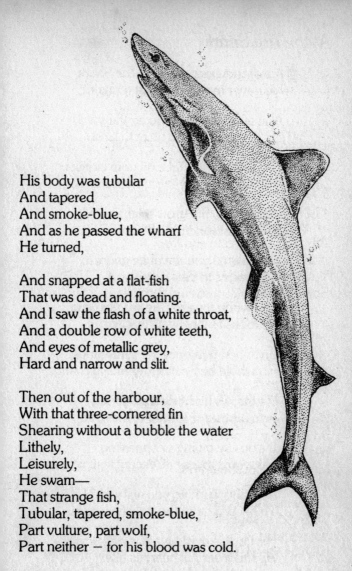

His body was tubular
And tapered
And smoke-blue,
And as he passed the wharf
He turned,

And snapped at a flat-fish
That was dead and floating.
And I saw the flash of a white throat,
And a double row of white teeth,
And eyes of metallic grey,
Hard and narrow and slit.

Then out of the harbour,
With that three-cornered fin
Shearing without a bubble the water
Lithely,
Leisurely,
He swam—
That strange fish,
Tubular, tapered, smoke-blue,
Part vulture, part wolf,
Part neither — for his blood was cold.

E. J. Pratt

The Shark

A treacherous monster is the Shark,
He never makes the least remark.

And when he sees you on the sand,
He doesn't seem to want to land.

He watches you take off your clothes,
And not the least excitement shows.

His eyes do not grow bright or roll,
He has astounding self-control.

He waits till you are quite undrest,
And seems to take no interest.

And when towards the sea you leap,
He looks as if he were asleep.

But when you once get in his range,
His whole demeanour seems to change.

He throws his body right about,
And his true character comes out.

It's no use crying or appealing,
He seems to lose all decent feeling.

After this warning you will wish
To keep clear of this treacherous fish.

His back is black, his stomach white,
He has a very dangerous bite.

Lord Alfred Douglas

A Narrow Fellow in the Grass

A narrow fellow in the grass
Occasionally rides;
You may have met him – did you not?
His notice sudden is.

The grass divides as with a comb,
A spotted shaft is seen,
And then it closes at your feet
And opens further on.

He likes a boggy acre,
A floor too cool for corn;
Yet when a child and barefoot,
I more than once at noon

Have passed, I thought, a whiplash
Upbraiding in the sun;
When, stooping to secure it,
It wrinkled and was gone.

Several of nature's people
I know, and they know me;
I feel for them a transport
Of cordiality,

But never met this fellow,
Attended or alone,
Without a tighter breathing
And zero at the bone.

Emily Dickinson

The Viper

Barefoot I went and made no sound;
The earth was hot beneath:
The air was quivering around,
The circling kestrel eyed the ground
And hung above the heath.

There in the pathway stretched along
The lovely serpent lay:
She reared not up the heath among,
She bowed her head, she sheathed her tongue,
And shining stole away.

Fair was the brave embroidered dress,
Fairer the gold eyes shone:
Loving her not, yet did I bless
The fallen angel's comeliness;
And gazed when she had gone.

Ruth Pitter

Snake

A snake came to my water-trough
On a hot, hot day, and I in pyjamas for the heat,
To drink there.

In the deep, strange-scented shade of the great dark
                                                carob-tree
I came down the steps with my pitcher
And must wait, must stand and wait, for there he was
                                    at the trough before me.

122

He reached down from a fissure in the earth-wall in
                the gloom
And trailed his yellow-brown slackness soft-bellied
            down, over the edge of the stone trough
And rested his throat upon the stone bottom,
And where the water had dripped from the tap, in a
                small clearness,
He sipped with his straight mouth,
Softly drank through his straight gums, into his slack
              long body,
Silently.

Someone was before me at my water-trough,
And I, like a second comer, waiting.

He lifted his head from his drinking, as cattle do,
And looked at me vaguely, as drinking cattle do,
And flickered his two-forked tongue from his lips, and
              mused a moment,
And stooped and drank a little more,
Being earth-brown, earth-golden from the burning
              bowels of the earth
On the day of Sicilian July, with Etna smoking.

The voice of my education said to me
He must be killed
For in Sicily the black, black snakes are innocent, the
              gold are venomous.
And voices in me said, If you were a man
You would take a stick and break him now, and finish
              him off.
But must I confess how I liked him,
How glad I was that he had come like a guest in quiet,
            to drink at my water-trough

And depart peaceful, pacified, and thankless,
Into the burning bowels of this earth?

Was it cowardice, that I dared not kill him?
Was it perversity, that I longed to talk to him?
Was it humility, to feel so honoured?
I felt so honoured.

And yet those voices:
If you were not afraid, you would kill him!

And truly I was afraid, I was most afraid,
But even so, honoured still more
That he should seek my hospitality
From out the dark door of the secret earth.

He drank enough
And lifted his head, dreamily, as one who has
                                    drunken,
And flickered his tongue like a forked night on the air,
                                    so black;
Seeming to lick his lips,
And looked around like a god, unseeing, into the air,
And slowly turned his head,
And slowly, very slowly, as if thrice adream,
Proceeded to draw his slow length curving round
And climb again the broken bank of my wall-face.

And as he put his head into that dreadful hole,
And as he slowly drew up, snake-easing his
                                    shoulders, and entered farther,
A sort of horror, a sort of protest against his
                        withdrawing into that horrid black hole,

Deliberately going into the blackness, and slowly
                              drawing himself after,
Overcame me now his back was turned.

I looked round, I put down my pitcher,
I picked up a clumsy log
And threw it at the water-trough with a clatter.

I think it did not hit him,
But suddenly that part of him that was left behind
                              convulsed in undignified haste,
Writhed like lightning, and was gone
Into the black hole, the earth-lipped fissure in the
                              wall-front,
At which, in the intense still noon, I stared with
                              fascination.

And immediately I regretted it.
I thought how paltry, how vulgar, what a mean act!
I despised myself and the voices of my accursed
                              human education.

And I thought of the albatross,
And I wished he would come back, my snake.
For he seemed to me again like a king,
Like a king in exile, uncrowned in the underworld,
Now due to be crowned again.

And so, I missed my chance with one of the lords
Of life.
And I have something to expiate;
A pettiness.

D. H. Lawrence

Snake

Suddenly the grass before my feet shakes and
becomes alive.
The snake
twists, almost leaps,
graceful even in terror,
smoothness looping back over smoothness
slithers away, disappears.
— And the grass is again still.
And surely, by whatever means of communication is
available to snakes,
the word is passed:
Hey, I just met a man, a monster, too;
Must have been, oh, seven feet tall.
So, keep away from the long grass,
it's dangerous there.

Ian Mudie

The Lizard

Little lizard, all alone,
Basking on that sunny stone,
Which you mask so cunningly,
You are very hard to see;
Still too as a stone you lie;
But I see a shining eye,
And I know that if I made
One step forward, like a shade
Quietly you would be gone,
Little spirit of the stone.

E. L. M. King

126

The Frog

Be kind and tender to the Frog,
   And do not call him names,
As 'Slimy-Skin', or 'Pollywog',
   Or likewise 'Uncle James',
Or 'Gape-a-grin', or 'Toad-gone-wrong',
   Or 'Billy Bandy-knees';
The frog is justly sensitive
   To epithets like these.

No animal will more repay
   A treatment kind and fair,
At least so lonely people say
Who keep a frog (and, by the way,
   They are extremely rare).

                              Hilaire Belloc

127

Earth-worm

Do
you
squirm
when
you
see
an earth-worm?
I never
do squirm
because I think
a big fat worm
is really rather clever
the way it can shrink
and go
so small
without
a sound
into the ground.
And then
what about
all
that
work it does
and no oxygen
or miner's hat?
Marvellous
you have to admit,
even if you don't like fat
pink worms a bit,
how with that
thin

slippery skin
it makes its way
day after day
through the soil,
such honest toil.
And don't forget
the dirt
it eats, I bet
you wouldn't like to come out
at night to squirt
it all over the place
with no eyes in your face:
I doubt
too if you know
an earth-worm is deaf, but
it can hear YOU go
to and fro
even if you cut
it in half.
So
do not laugh
or squirm
again
when
you
suddenly
see
a worm.

Leonard Clark

Upon the Snail

She goes but softly, but she goeth sure;
She stumbles not as stronger creatures do:
Her journey's shorter, so she may endure
Better than they which do much further go.

She makes no noise, but stilly seizeth on
The flower or herb appointed for her food,
The which she quietly doth feed upon,
While others range and gare, but find no good.

And though she doth but very softly go,
However 'tis not fast, nor slow, but sure;
And certainly they that do travel so,
The prize they do aim at, they do procure.

John Bunyan

Old Shellover

'Come!' said Old Shellover.
'What?' says Creep.
'The horny old Gardener's fast asleep;
The fat cock Thrush
To his nest has gone,
And the dew shines bright
In the rising Moon;
Old Sallie Worm from her hole doth peep;
Come!' said Old Shellover.
'Ay!' said Creep.

Walter de la Mare

The Microbe

The Microbe is so very small
You cannot make him out at all,
But many sanguine people hope
To see him through a microscope.
His jointed tongue that lies beneath
A hundred curious rows of teeth;
His seven tufted tails with lots
Of lovely pink and purple spots,
On each of which a pattern stands,
Composed of forty separate bands;
His eyebrows of a tender green;
All these have never yet been seen—
But Scientists, who ought to know,
Assure us that they must be so. . . .
Oh! let us never, never doubt
What nobody is sure about!

Hilaire Belloc

Four Little Things

There be four things which are little upon the earth
But they are exceeding wise;
The ants are a people not strong,
Yet they prepare their meat in the summer;
The conies are but a feeble folk,
Yet they make their houses in the rocks;
The locusts have no king,
Yet go they forth all of them by bands;
The spider taketh hold with her hands,
And is in kings' palaces.

The Book of Proverbs

The Ants

What wonder strikes the curious, while he views
   The black ant's city, by a rotten tree,
Or woodland bank! In ignorance we muse:
   Pausing, annoyed, − we know not what we see,
Such government and thought there seem to be;
Some looking on, and urging some to toil,
   Dragging their loads of bent-stalks slavishly:
And what's more wonderful, when big loads foil
   One ant or two to carry, quickly then
A swarm flock round to help their fellow-men.
   Surely they speak a language whisperingly,
Too fine for us to hear; and sure their ways
   Prove they have kings and laws, and that they be
Deformed remnants of the Fairy-days.

John Clare

Death of a Fly

Raising my pen to put a point
On the page, a dot over an i,
An unsteadily veering fly
Collides in a three-point landing, and settles.
Then, as if carving a joint,
It carefully sharpens its legs,
Sitting up the way a dog begs.
I notice a wing shed like a petal.
It had come here to die.
And my dot, streaked now with blood,
Turns the colour of mud.

Alan Ross

The Fly

How large unto the tiny fly
   Must little things appear!—
A rosebud like a feather bed,
   Its prickle like a spear;

A dewdrop like a looking-glass,
   A hair like golden wire;
The smallest grain of mustard-seed
   As fierce as coals of fire;

A loaf of bread, a lofty hill;
   A wasp, a cruel leopard;
And specks of salt as bright to see
   As lambkins to a shepherd.

Walter de la Mare

The Fly

Little Fly,
Thy summer's play
My thoughtless hand
Has brushed away.

Am not I
A fly like thee?
Or art not thou
A man like me?

For I dance,
And drink, and sing,
Till some blind hand
Shall brush my wing.

If thought is life
And strength and breath,
And the want
Of thought is death;

Then am I
A happy fly,
If I live
Or if I die.

William Blake

Autumn Glow-worm

A glow-worm underneath a dusky plume
Or canopy of yet unwithered fern,
Clear-shining, like a hermit's taper seen
Through a thick forest.

William Wordsworth

Ladybird

Tiniest of turtles!
Your shining back
Is a shell of orange
With spots of black.

How trustingly you walk
Across this land
Of hairgrass and hollows
That is my hand.

Your small wire legs,
So frail, so thin,
Their touch is swansdown
Upon my skin.

There! break out
Your wings and fly:
No tenderer creature
Beneath the sky.

Clive Sansom

World's End

Because, just then I'd nothing else to do,
I laid my chin upon the study table,
And watched a crack where the tough wood had split;
And, presently, there tumbled out of it,
A little beetle striped in green and blue.
Quickly he ran as fast as he was able
To the far end; then stopped, as though his wit
Had failed him there: and then as quickly flew,
With show of confidence incomparable,
Along the very edge, till seeing me there,
He stopped again; then peeps uneasy stole,
Down o'er the edge, which to him was world's end,
And then at me again that seemed no friend;
Next, longingly, across the table, where
His home showed safe. He knew not for his soul
What next to do: to run back, or to extend
Enquiry farther? – Then in sheer despair,
He gave it up, and scuttled to his hole.

G. K. Chettur

An August Midnight

A shaded lamp and a waving blind,
And the beat of a clock from a distant floor:
On this scene enter – winged, horned, and spined –
A longlegs, a moth, and a dumbledore;
While 'mid my page there idly stands
A sleepy fly, that rubs its hands. . . .

Thus meet we five, in this still place,
At this point of time, at this point in space.
— My guests besmear my new-penned line,
Or bang at the lamp and fall supine.
'God's humblest, they!' I muse. Yet why?
They know Earth-secrets that know not I.

Thomas Hardy

The Moth

Isled in the midnight air,
Musked with the dark's faint bloom,
Out into glooming and secret haunts
   The flame cries, 'Come!'

Lovely in dye and fan,
A-tremble in shimmering grace,
A moth from her winter swoon
   Uplifts her face:

Stares from her glamorous eyes;
Wafts her on plumes like mist;
In ecstasy swirls and sways
   To her strange tryst.

Walter de la Mare

Butterflies

Light as petals, white as daisies,
Shantung-cool in summer's blaze,
Butterflies through leaf-green mazes
Go their drunken, darling ways.

Nonchalantly in the sun they
Climb a dazzling height from where
Lightly, brightly, one by one, they
Tumble down the stems of air.—

Gay, erratic, wayward dancers,
Treading with a flippant grace
Airy polkas, fairy lancers
Down the polished floors of space.

Clive Sansom

Today I Saw the Dragon-fly

Today I saw the dragon-fly
Come from the wells where he did lie.

An inner impulse rent the veil
Of his old husk: from head to tail
Came out clear plates of sapphire mail.

He dried his wings: like gauze they grew;
Through crofts and pastures wet with dew
A living flash of light he flew.

Alfred Lord Tennyson

Grasshoppers

Grasshoppers go in many a thrumming spring
And now to stalks of tasselled sour-grass cling,
That shakes and sways a while, but still keeps straight;
While arching oxeye doubles with his weight.
Next on the cat-tail grass with farther bound
He springs, that bends until they touch the ground.

John Clare

Bumble-bee

In his black and yellow
Striped jersey he moves slowly
From flower to flower
Sucking out honey;
A fat and friendly fellow
Buzzing around me where
I am writing in the sun.

Before the house has awoken
And the Sunday rumbling
Of traffic has begun
The bumble-bee keeps bumbling
Among the flowers and tumbling
Drunk with honey
Round my table in the sun.

Douglas Gibson

The Wasp

When the ripe pears droop heavily,
The yellow wasp hums loud and long
His hot and drowsy summer song.
A yellow flame he seems to be,
When darting suddenly from high
He lights where fallen peaches lie.

Yellow and black – this tiny thing's
A tiger soul on elfin wings.

William Sharp

Hurt No Living Thing

Hurt no living thing,
  Ladybird nor butterfly,
Nor moth with dusty wing,
Nor cricket chirping cheerily,
Nor grasshopper, so light of leap,
  Nor dancing gnat,
  Nor beetle fat,
Nor harmless worms that creep.

Christina Rossetti

Index of titles

144

Index of first lines

149

150

Index of authors

Acknowledgements

The author and publishers would like to thank the following people for giving permission to include in this anthology material which is their copyright. The publishers have made every effort to trace copyright holders. If we have inadvertently omitted to acknowledge anyone we should be most grateful if this could be brought to our attention for correction at the first opportunity.

Barrie & Jenkins Limited for 'Night Song' by Frances Cornford, from *Collected Poems*, and for 'The Viper' by Ruth Pitter, published by The Cresset Press

The Bodley Head Limited for 'Mallard' by Rex Warner, from *Poems*

Boosey & Hawkes Music Publishers Limited for 'O What if the Fowler' by Charles Dalmon, from *Manx National Songs*

Edward Brathwaite for 'The Cat-eyed Owl', from *Talk of the Tamarinds*

Edward Calman for 'Shark' by Lord Alfred Douglas, from *Tails with a Twist*, published by Edward Arnold

Charles Causley and David Higham Associates Limited for 'My Mother Saw a Dancing Bear' by Charles Causley, from *Collected Poems*, published by Macmillan

Chatto & Windus Limited for 'Interruption to a Journey' by Norman MacCaig, from *Surroundings*

Robert A. Clark for 'Lion' and 'Earth-worm' by Leonard Clark

G. K. Chettier for 'World's End', from *Quicksilver Book 3*

John Robert Colombo for 'Riverdale Lion'

Constable Publishers for 'The Red Cockatoo', translated from the Chinese by Arthur Waley

Curtis Brown Limited, London, on behalf of The Estate of Roy Campbell, for 'The Zebras' from *Adamaster*

Curtis Brown Limited, New York, for 'The Hippopotamus' by Ogden Nash, from *I'm a Stranger Here Myself*

The Executors of the W. H. Davies Estate and Jonathan Cape Limited for 'The Rabbit' and 'Sheep' by W. H. Davies, from *Collected Poems*

157

Hodder & Stoughton Limited for 'The Leopards' by Bernard Spencer, from *With Luck Lasting*

Mrs Hodgson and Macmillan, London and Basingstoke, for 'The Bells of Heaven' and 'Stupidity Street' by Ralph Hodgson, from *Collected Poems*

Hughes Massie Limited for 'The Badgers' by Eden Phillpotts, from *The Beast*

Hutchinson Educational Limited for 'A London Sparrow's If' by J. A. Lindon, from *Billy the Kid*, edited by M. Baldwin

Richard Kell and Chatto & Windus Limited for 'Pigeons' by Richard Kell, from *Differences*

E. L. M. King for 'The Lizard'

James Kirkup and Oxford University Press for 'The Caged Bird in Springtime', from *A Spring Journey and Other Poems*

The Longman Group Limited for 'The Dromedary' by A. Y. Campbell, from *Poems*

George Macbeth for 'The Bird'

James MacGibbon for 'The Singing Cat' and 'Parrot' by Stevie Smith, from *The Collected Poems of Stevie Smith* published by Allen Lane

McGraw-Hill Ryerson Limited for 'The Goldfish' by A. A. Brown, from *All Fools' Day*

Macmillan, London and Basingstoke, for 'from Horses' by H. H. Abbott, from *Poetrycards*, edited by Gibson and Wilson; 'Skate' by Alan Brownjohn, from *Brownjohn's Beasts* and 'The Rabbit' by Alan Brownjohn, from *The Railings*; 'The Nightingale' by Ian Colvin, from *Rhyme and Rhythm*; and 'Goldfish' by John Walsh

Macmillan Publishing Co Inc for 'Something Told the Wild Geese' by Rachel Field, copyright 1934 by Macmillan Publishing Co Inc, renewed 1972 by Arthur S. Pederson

Barry Maybury for 'Horses' by Paddy Kinsale, from *Thought-shapes*

Methuen Children's Books for 'Death of a Fly' by Alan Ross, from *African Negatives*

Ian Mudie for 'Snake'

POETRY BOOKS

If you enjoyed all the poems in this book, why not read some more of our poetry collections, which are packed with poems for everyone to enjoy. They are available in bookshops or they can be ordered directly from us. Just complete the form below and send the right amount of money and the books will be sent to you at home.

☐ THE BEAVER BOOK OF SKOOL VERSE	Jennifer Curry (editor)	£1.25
☐ MORE SKOOL VERSE	Jennifer Curry (editor)	£1.50
☐ MARY HAD A CROCODILE	Jennifer Curry (editor)	£1.50
☐ THE BEAVER BOOK OF REVOLTING RHYMES	Jennifer and Graeme Curry (editors)	£1.25
☐ RHYME TIME	Barbara Ireson (editor)	£1.95
☐ RHYME TIME 2	Barbara Ireson (editor)	£1.95
☐ OVER AND OVER AGAIN	Barbara Ireson and Christopher Rowe	£1.50
☐ WITCHES' BREW	Ian and Zenka Woodward (editors)	£1.25
☐ IT'S FUNNY WHEN YOU LOOK AT IT	Colin West	£1.25
☐ THE LAND OF UTTER NONSENSE	Colin West	£1.25
☐ NOT TO BE TAKEN SERIOUSLY	Colin West	£1.00
☐ A STEP IN THE WRONG DIRECTION	Colin West	£1.00

If you would like to order books, please send this form, and the money due to:

ARROW BOOKS, BOOKSERVICE BY POST, PO BOX 29, DOUGLAS, ISLE OF MAN, BRITISH ISLES. Please enclose a cheque or postal order made out to Arrow Books Ltd for the amount due including 30p per book for postage and packing both for orders within the UK and for overseas orders.

NAME . . . .

ADDRESS . . . .

. . . .

Please print clearly.